# WHAT SHALL WE DO AT GRANDMA'S HOUSE?

A Book of Ideas and Easy Activities for
Grandparents and their Young
Grandchildren

By

Jean Tuemmler

The author, Jean Tuemmler, is a credentialed
Early Childhood teacher who taught and directed
preschool for 15 years. She is a home economist
and has taught children's art and cooking classes.

Her first book was The Magic Oven,
a microwave cookbook for children.

She and her husband, Fred, have raised two
terrific sons, who with their wives have produced
two granddaughters and two grandsons. This
book is a result of her time spent with children,
and also sharing ideas with her many, many,
grand parenting friends.

# Preface

One of life's great pleasures is becoming a grandparent. The special relationship between you and your grandchildren is unlike any other. It can be delightful and rewarding. It can also be a challenge, especially if the last children you played with were your own. How will you entertain these little people when they come to visit you? Here are some answers to the question "What shall we do at Grandma's house today?"

This book is designed to suggest ideas for interacting with young children using simple activities. It is divided into several areas; art, science, music, cooking, dance, drama, outings, stories and games. There are ideas for active and quiet times, all planned for adults who are not used to spending time with children, but who want to share their quality time and unconditional love.

In addition to the activities I have suggested, I especially want to encourage all grandparents to share your passion with your grandchildren, whatever it is: yoga, tennis, baking, fishing, drawing, hiking, reading, knitting or traveling. One Grampa I know is passionate about baseball. His grandchildren have gone to games with him since they were two, and their favorite song is "Take Me Out to the Ballgame"! To show a child what delights you is to double your own delight.

Preparing your home for a visit

Whether your little grandchildren are regular visitors or you only see them a few times a year, some preparations will be needed. Naturally you will want to put away the glass nick-nacks and doo-dads and the antique tea set. Also please move cleaning supplies and other potentially dangerous substances to an upright and locked position. Don't tempt fate.

You don't need to buy a lot of toys. Some simple things your own children liked are still great favorites with little boys and girls. Legos (in the larger size) and a Brio train set with the simple wooden tracks, and maybe a few little trucks and your beanie baby collection is really all you need. A few little toy people (Playmobil makes nice ones) and a good set of wooden blocks make a nice addition, and will allow for maximum use of imagination in their play. Be very wary of toys with small pieces, which could cause choking.

If you have a big box or a lower drawer that can be emptied to become the toy drawer, your grandchildren will know just where to go to find their things whenever they come to see you.

They will most likely bring along their current favorite toys to show you and to play with.

You will need to keep a child car seat whenever you have a child under 60 lbs. visiting. Even if you don't plan to drive

anywhere, you may need it in an
emergency.

It will help to have a sturdy stepstool for
the child to use when helping you in the
kitchen, and also for washing hands in
the bathroom. Speaking of bathrooms, it
is worthwhile to invest in a potty seat that
can fit on your toilet.

It's a good idea to also have a change of
clothes for children of any age, for messy
artwork or water play, but especially for
the young ones. And, of course, you'll
need a package of diapers for the babies
and toddlers.

There are some things you might normally
throw away that you could start to save
for a rainy day project with the kids.
These would be cardboard tubes from
paper towels or wrapping paper. (These
can turn into a variety of things such as
telescopes, scarecrows, scepters, and
swords.) Pretty shiny gold and silver
papers can be used in collages, and small
cardboard boxes are great for building
towers. (See art chapter.) Of course any
time you have a big appliance box you
have an almost ready-made playhouse.
Just cut a few windows and doors!

<u>A word about Grand-names:</u>
One special thing we get with our first
grandchild is a new name...our 'grand'
name! You may actually have a say in
what it will be. 'Grandma' and 'Grandpa'
are real favorites, of course, but what if
the baby's other grandparents are already
using those names, or what if you prefer
something more unique?

The names by which your children refer to
you are the names the babies will learn to
call you. So let them know at once if you
have a preference. One little girl had not
referred to her grandmother by name until
she was two. One morning she saw her
grandmother and said "Good Morning,
Darlin". That was her name thereafter.
Don't you love Grandpa and Darlin?

Nana, Nonna, Ooma and Oopa have a
European flavor, and may fit into your
family heritage. Granny, Grampy, Mimi,
Poppa, Pappy, Grandmom and Grandad
are popular, and the variations, which
occur with the grandbaby's interesting
pronounciation: How do you like Pooba,
Mamoo, Boopa, Damma and Dadoo.

This book is dedicated to Andrea, Frederick, Kathryn and Forrest, my inspirations.

# Table of Contents

The bond between child and grandparent can indeed be the purest, least complicated form of human love.

# YOU MADE IT! LET'S EAT!

Even very little children can enjoy sharing the kitchen with Nana. Not only do children love to be with you in the kitchen, they nearly always love to eat what they have created.

And as they stir and add ingredients they can learn about healthy food. Where does milk come from? How does a carrot grow? What makes bread rise?

Some precautions:
Always be sure that an adult handles the heat source. Don't worry too much about little spills or fingers tasting the dough. You will find the cooking experience worth the extra work that's involved. Be sure that children wash their hands before starting and are included in the cleanup too. Here are some suggestions for cooking and kitchen activities, always with good nutrition and health in mind.

KITCHEN PLAY

Dishwashing (Age 1½ +)
Even the very youngest ones can wash plastic dishes in the sink. Have a secure step stool or a kitchen chair turned backwards at the sink. A towel folded under the stool is a good idea too, to prevent slipping. Fill the sink with a few inches of warm soapy water and add funnels, small plastic pitchers for pouring practice, cups, ladles, wooden spoons and

brushes. Tie a tea towel around the child's middle to soak up some of the water. Stand back!

Food Washing (age 2+)
When you bring in the harvest from your vegetable garden or the supermarket, the produce can use a good scrubbing. A small brush and dishpan and a grandchild can help! Again, use a secure stepstool if you have one, and be near the child at the sink, or you can put a dishpan on a low table.

Cupboard Chaos (Age 1 ½ )
I hope you have a low accessible cupboard or drawer where you keep your Tupperware containers and other fun stuff. You probably remember how much your own children liked to empty, sort and generally bang around in there. This is usually good for 10 minutes or so of entertainment for a toddler while you are trying to do something in the kitchen.

Rice Play (Age 2+)
Find a large metal or plastic container. A turkey roaster is ideal. Empty into it a 2 pound bag of rice. Just add spoons, ladles, measuring cups, funnels, and pitchers. Set it on the floor or a low table where cleanup is easy, and your little explorers can make roads, practice filling, pouring, and scooping. Rice can be cleaned and reused of course. Other things that can be used in this way are birdseed, lentils, and unpopped popcorn. If you have a natural food store with bins

of grains you might find a dry ingredient you like even better.

Dippity Do (Age 2+)
I have found that children love to dip food. As a matter of fact, most people do, don't you? Here are some healthy things to serve to small people:

Banana slices to dip into finely ground granola, or sesame seeds,

Melon cubes or strawberries to dip into yogurt,

Fat free hotdogs (cut lengthwise first for safety) to dip into ketchup,

Crisp breadsticks to dip into peanut butter,

Toast "fingers'" can dip into apple butter or flavored yogurt,

Pita bread triangles to dip into hummus or guacamole,

Shrimps to dip into cocktail sauce.

Because of the chance of very little ones choking, the following are recommended for children over three:

Raw veggies of all kinds to dip. Not just carrot sticks! Cut up peppers, jicama, broccoli, sugar snap peas, cauliflower, or mushrooms, to dip into cottage cheese flavored with a little ranch dressing or soy sauce.

BREAKFAST IDEAS

French Toast (Age 3+)
  With a fork, children can stir together 2
  eggs and ¾ cup milk for French toast. Mix
  with a fork until well blended (all one
  color). Add a few drops of vanilla. Your
  grandchild can dip day-old bread into it
  and watch while you cook it with a little
  butter. She can also sprinkle it with
  cinnamon sugar. Top with maple syrup,
  sweetened yogurt, or applesauce.

Pancakes (Children can help you mix and stir at age
4+)
  Pancakes are always fun to eat. When you
  make them for the family, here are some
  variations you can do for the children's
  enjoyment:

  - You can make the pancakes in the
    shape of each child's initial.
  - Shape them into funny animals,
    snakes, butterflies.
  - Add a small amount of food coloring
    to the batter.
  - Add chopped apples, blueberries,
    sweetened dried cranberries or
    chopped bananas to the batter.
  - Offer a squeeze bottle of honey,
    peanut butter, or apple butter for
    toppings, instead of maple syrup.

  Here is a good family recipe if you don't
  have one of your own.

Buttermilk Pancakes
2 ½ cups buttermilk
3 eggs, beaten
3 tablespoons canola oil or melted butter

2 cups flour (use part whole wheat if you
have it)
1 teaspoon baking soda
1½ teaspoons baking powder
½ teaspoon salt
2 tablespoons sugar

Mix the eggs and milk and blend well. Mix
the dry ingredients in another bowl and
whisk them together. Let grandchildren
stir the dry ingredients until they are
tired. Add 3 tablespoons oil or melted
butter to the liquids and stir again.
Stir into the dry ingredients, just until
blended.

Cook on a hot, nonstick griddle.

(Or you can use a prepared mix. Krusteaz
is good, easy and healthy.)

Applesauce (Any age can enjoy it)
Cut an apple around the equator
(crosswise). See the little star in the
middle made by seeds? Remove the apple
core and seeds. Grandchildren can now
cut the apple into pieces with a safe knife.
(Plastic knives with serration work well
enough and won't cut small fingers.)

Notice how the hard chunks of apples
turn into "mush" as it cooks. One apple
(peeled or not) cut into small chunks and
placed in a small dish, can cook into

applesauce in just a couple of minutes in the microwave. Add a bit of honey or brown sugar if you like and stir with a cinnamon stick to cool it.

WHAT'S FOR LUNCH?
When the grandchildren are staying for lunch, it is fun to include them in the preparations. Fruit flavored yogurt and string cheese seem to be two universal favorites. Here are some other easy ideas.

Tuna Sandwich (Age 3+)
Open and drain a can of tuna. A child can smash and stir it in a little bowl with mayo, relish, and some grated apple for a delicious sandwich. Spread it on toast or fill ½ of a pita bread for a "tuna boat".

Nut Butter (Age 3 Or 4+)
Spreading peanut butter can be difficult for little hands. It helps to soften the PB in the microwave for a few seconds and stir it up. Let children spread it on toasted bread or apple slices, whole-wheat crackers, or fill celery sticks.

Decorate your sandwich or snack with raisins to make "frogs on a log".

Slices of banana on an open-face peanut butter sandwich are also fun and delicious. Kids can cut the banana into "coin" slices with a plastic serrated knife. How about banana eyes and a raisin smile?

Try other nut butters: almond, cashew and soy are all tasty.

Egg Salad (3+)
Cook and cool hardboiled eggs. Let the kids try to peel their own. (They may need help here.) With a serrated plastic knife, cut the egg in half and place flat side down on a plate. Smash into small bits with a sturdy fork, and add mayo and a small amount of salt and pepper to taste. Spread on whole-wheat crackers or toast.

Fruit Smoothies (Age 2+)
Into your blender, let the kids put ½ banana, ½ cup orange juice, ½ cup plain or vanilla yogurt or frozen yogurt and 3 strawberries or some other fresh fruit. Put the top of the blender on tight and let her buzz 20 seconds. Yumm. This makes enough for two small smoothies.

Fruit Salad (Age 4+)
Using the serrated plastic knife again, children can cut bananas, mandarin orange segments, a pineapple ring, strawberries, grapes, and/or melon slices into small pieces. Stir and stir. Top with fruit or vanilla yogurt if the children like it. Make enough for everybody!!

Soft Tacos Or Quesadillas
These are fun for kids to "build" on a tortilla. Place a tortilla on a paper plate. Kids can choose their toppings: grated cheese is a favorite topping of course, and older children can grate it (careful of the knuckles!). Prepared salsa, cubed avocados, sliced tomatoes, shredded

lettuce and scallions if you like, can all pile on top. Even scrambled eggs! "Nuke" each tortilla on a paper plate in the microwave oven for 30 seconds, or so, to melt the cheese. Let it cool a few minutes. Fold it over and enjoy.

Personal Pizza (3+)
Here's a meal my grandsons love! Give each child a 5-6 inch uncooked pizza crust on an oiled square of aluminum foil. (Use pre-prepared (Boboli), or frozen bread dough or the simple recipe, which follows.) The kids can do some of the preparation of the toppings here, according to age and ability:
- Have dishes of grated cheese, sliced olives, cut-up mushrooms, tomato sauce and maybe some meat or sausage slices. The grandkids can create their own feast.
- Set the foil squares on a baking sheet at 400° until crust is brown and toppings are bubbly. (About 12-15 minutes.) LET IT COOL a few minutes. Enjoy! This is fun for a larger group of children too. The only hard part is waiting for the pizzas to cook.

Pizza crusts: In food processor: combine 3 cups all purpose flour, 1 pkg. dry yeast, 1 tablespoon olive oil, 1 teaspoon salt, and blend. With processor running, add 1 cup very warm water. Let processor mix for 1 minute. The dough should be smooth and soft. Divide into 6-8 portions and flatten to

make individual pizzas. Proceed as above, or make one big one if you want.
Simpler version: use ½ English muffin as base.

Cheese Pretzels (4+)
Baking with yeast is an experience every young cook should have. The smell of freshly baked bread is irresistible and the fun of seeing dough rise as the yeast "grows" is a fascinating lesson. The pretzel recipe is good for four or five-year-old's first try and tasty enough to serve to company.

You will need:

1 pkg. active dry yeast
1½ cups warm water
1 tsp salt
1 tablespoon sugar
4 cups flour
8 oz. cheddar cheese, grated
1 beaten egg + 1 tablespoon water

Wash all hands.
Preheat oven to 425°. In a large bowl dissolve yeast in water. Stir in salt and sugar. Stir in flour and grated cheese. (Save ½ cup of the flour for later use in case dough is sticky.) Knead dough until smooth. Form a big log, cut

in half and half again until you have 16
pieces. Roll each into a long rope or snake.
Twist into shape. (Be prepared to see some
very un-pretzel-like shapes). Place on cookie
sheets and brush with the beaten egg.
Sprinkle salt on top if desired. Bake 15
minutes or until golden brown.

Frozen bread dough can be used to make
pretzels and also the pizza dough if you aren't
interested in baking from scratch. It is super
easy and the whole wheat version is healthy
too.

Ironed Cheese Sandwich
  Here's a switch! You will need an iron for
  this one. An adult should handle the hot
  iron. Lay a large square of aluminum foil
  on a breadboard. Butter two pieces of
  bread and lay one on the foil (butter side
  down) and top it with your favorite kind of
  cheese. Put the other piece of bread on the
  cheese, butter side up. Cover the
  sandwich with another piece of foil. Iron
  the foil with a hot iron for a few minutes
  on each side. This will toast the bread and
  melt the cheese.

Bulging Baked Potato
  Overflowing with vitamins and good flavor,
  this makes a great lunch. Make one potato
  for each person if they are small potatoes,
  cut them in half if they are the big ones.

  Wash a potato under warm water to clean
  it well. Poke 3 or 4 holes in it. Place in
  microwave on a paper towel. Cook 2
  minutes at full power. Turn it over and
  cook 2 minutes more, or until it feels soft

when you poke it. Let it rest while you find good things to put in it. How about butter, shredded cheese, steamed broccoli, chopped ham, tuna, or chopped green onions. Slit it open and fill with the goodies.

If you prefer to cook in a regular oven, bake at 400° about 45-50 minutes or until done.

## SWEET TREATS

I'm sure you have a tried and true cookie recipe that your grandchildren will eagerly help you make. In addition to your own family favorites, here are a few ideas for hands-on cookie making.

### Scottish Shortbread
Help mix soft butter (1 stick) with sugar (1/4 cup) and flour 1¼ cups) for Scottish shortbreads. With very clean hands, pat the dough flat and even into an 8" or 9" round cake pan and score into wedges with a fork. Have your grandchild count how many cookies that will make. (8-12) Ask the child, " Is that enough?" Bake at 325° for 40 minutes.

### Baked Apple
Try this for breakfast or dessert.
Peel and core a tasty apple. (An adult will need to do this part.) Put it in a custard cup or small dish. Fill the center hole with a chunk of butter and 2 spoonfuls of brown sugar. Sprinkle with cinnamon and nutmeg. Wrap the dish in waxed paper or

plastic wrap. Cook in microwave oven about 3 minutes on full power. Let stand to cool.

Fruit Leather
    You will need:
    2 cups fresh fruit, washed, pitted, and chopped
    2 tablespoons sugar or honey
    1 tablespoon lemon juice

Choose berries, peaches, apples, plums, or whatever you like.
Puree prepared fruit in a blender with small amount of water to make a smooth puree. You may add 2 or 3 tablespoons of honey or sugar to sweeten if necessary.
Add 1 tablespoon lemon juice to prevent darkening. Stir.

Line a cookie sheet with waxed paper sprayed with cooking spray. Spread puree ½ inch thick and dry in very low oven (120°) overnight, or outside in the hot sun on a summer day. Cover with cheesecloth to keep the bugs off if its outside. When leathery to the touch, peel off the paper and place on plastic wrap, and roll up.

Brown Sugar Cinnamon Cutouts
    These crisp cookies are the simplest and the best! Little kids can roll out and cut the dough into animals or holiday shapes. The recipe makes lots of dough, and it can be frozen in an airtight bag for future use if you don't use it all.

You will need:

    1 lb. brown sugar (light or dark)
    1 lb. butter at room temperature
    4½ cups all-purpose flour
    1 teaspoon cinnamon
    1 ½ teaspoons vanilla

Cream the sugar, butter, and vanilla in large bowl of your mixer until fluffy. Work in cinnamon and flour at slow speed. Form dough into a ball and wrap airtight in plastic. Chill an hour or up to a week. Let dough come to room temperature before rolling it out.

Wash hands. Preheat oven to 300°. Pinch off small amounts of dough and roll out to about ¼ inch thick on floured board, and cut into shapes. Place on ungreased cookie sheets and bake at 300° for about 15 minutes or until slightly browned. Let cool 3 minutes on cookie sheet and then move to a rack to cool completely.

Gingerbread House

Decorating a gingerbread house can be a wonderful, creative and magical experience for children.

Assemble the basic cookie house well in advance of the grand kids' arrival, because the actual building (putting up the walls and the roof) is sometimes tricky, and the icing glue needs to be dry before the decorating itself can start.

There are two ways to go here. You can purchase the cookie house sections in a kit, and assemble them with the icing glue. If you are a baker you can certainly bake the gingerbread sections and assemble them. It is important to have a sturdy cardboard base to build it on, which can also be decorated.

One little friend made her house into a barn and added the animals. I have made a Noah's Ark with my gingerbread and added the animals two-by-two. This year my grandsons decorated a gingerbread train, with a box car full of cookies. Use your imagination and involve the children in the planning stage as well as the creation of the masterpiece.

Here is the recipe for Royal Icing, which acts as glue.

<u>Royal Icing</u>

1 cup confectioners' sugar
¼ teaspoon cream of tartar
1 egg white
1/3 cup boiling water
Combine these in a medium bowl and beat until icing holds stiff peaks. Generously apply along the adjoining sides and hold the walls upright while the icing hardens. Repeat with remaining sides and finally the roof. Let icing harden well before decorating. A really easy way to direct the icing is to spoon icing into a small plastic sandwich bag and snip off a tiny piece of the corner. You can squeeze the bag and get a nice stream of icing. Easy cleanup!

Some decorating ideas: Necco wafers for roof tiles, tiny candy canes for a door frame, life savers for windows, red jellybellies along the peak of the roof. Please wash hands first and brush teeth after this project.

Frozen Bananas
1 Banana
2 Popsicle sticks

optional entertainment:
melted peanut butter
toasted sunflower seeds
melted chocolate
melted caramel
chopped nuts

Peel a firm banana. Cut it in half lengthwise and insert a stick into end of each half. Wrap in plastic and freeze. Eat as is, or dip into honey or peanut butter or melted chocolate or caramel, and then into seeds or chopped nuts.

---

*Chocolate Cake*

*Chocolate chips*
*Sugar*
*Apple*
*Spaghetti*
*Grapes*
*Put it all into the mixer*
*Then you fold it up*
*Cook it 30 minutes.*

*Rebecca Gordon,*
*Age 2 1/2*

---

Rice Crispy Treats
Generally I like to avoid sticky sweet treats for kids, but these are so universally loved I've included this recipe, with fun, easy new directions.

6 cups of crisp rice cereal or another crunchy cereal or a combination of the two.
1 (10 oz.) bag (about 40) marshmallows
3 tablespoons butter or margarine

Put the butter and marshmallows in a big, preferably glass, mixing bowl. Put the bowl in the microwave and cook on full power about 2 minutes. The marshmallows will grow and puff up like magic. Stir the melted marshmallow with the butter, and add the cereal. Mix with a big spoon and press with damp hands into a 9"x13" pan which has been sprayed with cooking spray.
Get creative! Stir in some pine nuts or toasted sunflower seeds, dried fruit bits, mini chocolate chips or M&Ms. Or maybe just some pretty sprinkles.

Warm Cinnamon Cider
Pour apple juice into a mug. Add a cinnamon stick. Heat for 1½ minutes in the microwave and stir with the cinnamon stick until cool enough to drink.

Ffffruitcicles
Using concentrated fruit juice, dilute with only half the water called for on the can. Pour into tiny paper cups and cover the tops with plastic wrap. Place them in a baking pan, for easy transporting. Poke a popsicle stick through the middle of theplastic so it will stand up in the cup. Place in freezer overnight.
To remove the fruitcicles, dip the cup into warm water for a few seconds.

# QUIET TIMES

There are so many important lessons we can learn from our grandchildren. The most important is to listen well to them. As grandparents, most of us have the pleasure and the luxury of not having to hurry through life and so we can take time to hear their stories, dreams and concerns.

READ ME A STORY

Snuggling on the sofa together with a warm child and a book is one of a grandparent's greatest joys. I have found that having a special drawer or shelf for the children's books is a great help. They know just where to go and make their choices quickly.

You don't need a lot of books: you'll find that a few special ones are chosen over and over again. As the book becomes more familiar, children often are able to fill in words when you leave them out. Use the reading opportunity to ask the child questions about the story or relate the story to your or your grandchild's life.

Some classics that have been popular, probably since you were a child, are:

- Pokey Little Puppy
- The Little Engine that Could
- Gingerbread Boy
- Ferdinand
- Goodnight Moon
- The Very Hungry Caterpillar
- Bread and Jam for Frances

The Dr. Seuss books are fun to read aloud and are always a favorite with children.

As the children get older they will be ready for "chapter books". This means less pictures and more story. One good series to start with is 'The Magic Treehouse". The adventures that the children have in the stories are interesting, fun and educational.

Baby Books

In our family I have created a scrapbook for each grandchild when he/she was born. Each starts with a few pictures of the family before the baby arrived. ("They were waiting for you.") The first footprint and hospital photos are next, with the birth announcement and then snapshots of the baby being held by various family members. The cards of congratulations and pictures of the first outings with Nana and Grandpa are included, and shots of the baby's growth and highlights of the first year. The books gradually end after the first birthday. All of the children delight in revisiting their baby books over and over again. Katie likes to see the book of "When I was very tiny".

Family Pictures

You are the link between the past and the future for your grandkids. Dig out the pictures of your parents and grandparents and tell the stories you remember about going to your own grandma's house when you were little. Were there some family traditions that you would like to pass down to a new generation? See if you can detect family resemblances between the generations. Sketch a simple family tree and try to fill the names on the twigs and branches for at least four generations. If you can add the pictures to the family tree that is even better!

> *To our grandchildren, what we tell them about their parents' childhood and our own young years is living history.*
>
> *Ruth Goode*
> *American Writer (b 1905)*

TELL ME A STORY

Stories only you can tell, about what happened when you were small, are stories the children will remember all their lives. What were your favorite toys, and who were your best friends? What was your family like? Did you walk to school? Tell about your house and your car and your neighborhood. There have been so many changes just in daily life since your childhood, that must seem pretty amazing to young ones.

Our eldest granddaughter, at three, always needed a story before bed...an original story about some event in the life of a toy or animal or relative of her choosing. Fun as this is, it can be a challenge! Say, "Let's do it this way. I'll start the story off with a few sentences and then stop midway through a sentence for you to finish the thought. When you stop, I'll add some more." Who knows where this story will go?

The classic stories you remember from your childhood are fun to tell over and over too. We want the little ones to hear the classics, right? Remember:

- The Three Bears
- Little Red Riding Hood
- The Three Little Pigs
- Peter Pan
- The Billy Goats Gruff

If you don't remember all the details, find a collection at the library or bookstore.

SLEEPY TIME

Some little children can sleep just about anywhere. Most, though, are sensitive enough to different surroundings that special thought should go into preparing so they feel safe and secure. When the grandchildren, and their parents are ready for a sleepover, plan ahead.

The children should arrive with plenty of time to acclimate to the new location before it is time for bed.

One of my granny friends has her little granddaughters camp out in sleeping bags on her bedroom floor so if they wake up in the night there is someone comforting right there for them. I remember sleeping between my grandparents in their bed when I was about 3 years old. At least one book before bedtime is probably a must to form the warm comforting bond.

Our grandchildren drift off to sleep with a favorite CD playing their familiar sleepy music, and of course their familiar 'lovey' or favorite blanket.

A CD of quiet lullabies is a great relaxer for nap times too.

Back Rubs

Don't forget the relaxing power of a good back rub. Most children really enjoy back-rubs, and often in a specific way. "Just rub up and down, not around." Or "just scratch, don't pat". During nap time or sleepovers back rubs are very comforting. Some times we take turns rubbing each other's back. "You do mine and I'll do yours."

Interactive Videos

Even though I like to avoid TV for little children, sometimes a video is just the thing for quiet time after dinner. A big bowl of popcorn is always fun too. (Only for children with plenty of molars. Very young ones might choke on it.)

My favorites for young children are the old Disney Classic animated films such as Fantasia, Snow White, Bambi, Cinderella, Lady and the Tramp, Dumbo, etc. Also great favorites for young children are Madeline, Theodore Tugboat, Sound of Music, Mary Poppins and Annie. Please watch with them, sitting next to or under them as they watch. Even these shows have some scary parts and it is good to have a warm adult to talk to about them.

> *What is so simple even a small child can manipulate it?*
> *A grandparent.*
> *-anonymous*

## LONG-DISTANCE GRANDPARENTING

Here are a few ideas for those grandparents who, like us, have grandchildren who live far away. Regular telephone calls can be started even before the child is really talking well. He can learn to love hearing Grandma's voice for a short phone visit, and will soon be chatting back. (You may need an interpreter at first.)

Books On Tape

Our grandsons live across the country from us. One of the ways we have tried to keep in touch between visits is to send them books, each month, with a tape recording of our voices reading the book, which we also send. We hope they remember Nana and Boopa's voices as they listen to the story and turn the pages.

Snail Mail Notes
Send a bundle of self-addressed, stamped envelopes and blank note cards to your far-away grandchild. He can draw a picture or write a note any time and send it off to you. Even if he is only in the next town.

> Grandchildren are the dots that connect the lines from generation to generation.

You've Got E-Mails!
Chances are that by the time your grandchildren are in school, they will be quite comfortable and proficient with the computer. What a wonderful and easy way to stay in touch. And with Web Cams now you can also see each other as you chat online.

Grandma And Grandpa Dolls
If you have some basic sewing skills and you have access to a scanner, you can scan full color pictures of yourselves on to transfer paper (available at craft supply stores) and iron the images onto white cotton. Cut them out to sew and stuff to make little dolls. Why not make dolls of the whole family?

Magnetic Grand Parents or Why is Grandpa stuck to the refrigerator?
One of my clever grandmother friends suggested this nifty idea. Buy a roll of

magnetic sheet at the craft store or office supply. It is a flexible black material that sticks like a magnet to metal. Choose full-length pictures of Grandma, Grandpa, and/or the children. (6-10 inches high works best.) Attach the pictures to the magnetic sheet according to the package directions and cut around each figure to make a "paper-doll" that the children can stick to the fridge at their house. Now they have you to play with all the time.

# LITTLE ARTISTS

## PREPARING YOUR ART CENTER

First, hide the Sharpee pens and other permanent markers.

Prepare a drawer, cupboard or even a shoebox of art supplies for the exclusive use of your young artists. It could include washable markers, crayons, children's scissors, tape, stickers, watercolors, papers and envelopes. My family room also has a small table and chairs so the children can, and do, work independently.

As you watch the art being produced try saying "Tell me about your picture," instead of asking, " What is that?" This change will enable your grandchild to expand on his or her thinking and encourage language development. Write her description as a caption to the picture. You might get a wonderful story. If you save the masterpieces, (especially the self portraits) be sure to label and date each one. Before she can write her name, ask the child where on the picture she would like her name printed.

## HOME MADE PLAYDOUGH
I like this so much better than the chemical-smelling kind you can buy. The first time you make it you might want to prepare it before the kids come.

This makes a fragrant, pastel playdough that will last months in a plastic bag in the fridge. It feels especially good in your hands when it is warm from the pan.

You will need:
1 cup flour
¼ cup salt
3 oz. pkg. Jello
1 cup water
2 tablespoons cream of tartar

Mix all ingredients together in a heavy saucepan. Stir over medium heat for 3-5 minutes until dough begins to form and is no longer sticky. Turn out onto a lightly floured surface and knead until smooth. Store in an airtight container.

I like to let little hands create their own shapes (snakes, balls, snowmen, cookies) before pulling out the cookie cutters. Find some small dowels for rolling the dough flat and then press interesting shapes in to the dough; anything washable such as leaves, forks, keys, little hands, make interesting impressions. And then of course, there are the seasonal cookie cutters. You can keep the dough in an airtight bag in the fridge for months, and it will retain its nice texture.

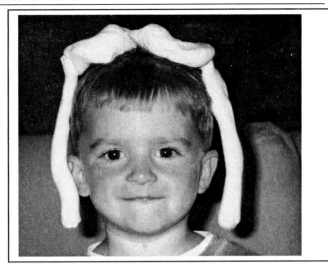

ART CLAY

This is white dough that becomes very hard when it dries. When dry, it can be painted and lacquered and used to make permanent creations for gifts such as: children's handprints or pendants. Children can create collages of seeds, acorns, cones, or shells, dipped into white glue and pressed into the dough.

You will need:

1 cup cornstarch
2 cups baking soda
1 ¼ cup cold water

Combine in a heavy saucepan and heat gradually, stirring, until the mixture becomes like mashed potatoes. Turn out on a board and knead until smooth. It can be crumbly, so for stability, press the dough into a flat plastic lid and then create the handprint, or nature collage.

Keep clay covered in an airtight bag until you want it to harden. It will harden overnight if left out at room temperature.

EASY MIX PLAYDOUGH
This is easy for children to mix up.
¼ cup of warm water
¼ cup of salt
1 teaspoon oil
few drops of food coloring
½ cup flour + 2 tablespoons
Stir these together in the order listed.
Knead on a floured surface until smooth.
Store in a plastic bag.

WATERCOLORS
I have a simple set of watercolors (6 colors each) for each grandchild. I give them each a small plastic cup of water and several brushes and assorted paper. The children all love this and they each started at about age 2 ½. The results have been wonderful. Our favorite place to paint is on a small plastic table outside in the patio. We have found the wooden stairway a perfect spot for drying the paintings.

An interesting variation is box painting. Save a collection of small cardboard boxes that the children can paint. They may turn out to be houses, treasure chests, castles, or who knows? Try using toilet paper tubes, coffee filters, or any kind absorbent paper or cardboard. These can be taped or stapled or glued together and then painted.

FINGERPAINTING

Feeling brave? This works best outside on a nice day but can be lots of fun indoors too. The trick is to have a tray or cookie sheet with sides to contain the paint. My favorite "paint" to use is simply shaving cream. Sometimes children are reluctant to get their hands messy, but if you show them they can start with one finger, then one hand, then stand back! This might be a good time for the kitchen towel around the middle of the child. You will want to add a drop or two of food coloring. How about foot painting outside on a hot day?

This activity can also be moved to the bathtub at bath time.

A slightly messier version, but more delicious, is to offer chocolate pudding as the fingerpaint. This time of course the hands that participate must be very clean.

SIDEWALK CHALK
I know you are familiar with the fat chalks
designed for use on driveways and patios.
Children learning their letters and
numbers can really enjoy this "play". The
best part is after your yard is thoroughly
decorated with pictures and letters and
names, a quick jet spray from the hose
cleans it all up.

WATERPLAY
This is a wonderful activity for even very
young children and they never seem to tire
of it.

Put water in a bucket or tub outside on a
warm day. Add a small amount of liquid
detergent if you want to. Equipment that's
fun to use: sponges, funnels, squirt
bottles, eggbeaters, and lots of plastic
containers, small pitchers and cups. They
can wash rubber dolls, balls, and rocks.
They can "paint" fences, decks, walls with
inexpensive brushes and a can of water.
Add an old scrub brush and scrub the
bricks or flagstones. My granddaughters
like to pretend they are the Cinderellas,
and are scrubbing the stones for the ugly
stepmother.

STRINGING STUFF
Make necklaces by stringing dry noodles
with holes in them, cut-up plastic straws,
beads, or buttons, on stiff heavy thread,
dental floss, or string. (This can be
frustrating if the end of the string frays, so
dip the end of the string into white glue

and let dry in preparation, or wrap the end in masking tape.) Don't have any expectations about how many beads, or in what order they go when the children are little. The concept of sorting, ordering, and patterning comes with age. The string for each child should be long enough to go easily over the head. Start by tying a bead on the far end of the string, so the others won't fall off.

In preparation you may want to color macaroni or noodles...(any kind with a hole through it.) Put 2 tablespoons of rubbing alcohol in a jar with a lid. Add a few drops of food coloring (use a separate jar for each color.) Put in a handful of pasta and shake. Lift noodles out with a spoon onto paper towels to dry. They won't get sticky, and will dry fast.

BUBBLE ART

You will need a quart jar or tall glass. Put in 2 tablespoons of dishwashing detergent (Dawn works best), 1 tablespoon of water and ½ teaspoon of food coloring. Put a long plastic drinking straw into the jar and blow. Colored bubbles will form and overflow the jar. If you scoop them onto a piece of paper, a beautiful design will form as the bubbles pop. Be sure the bubble-blower understands the concept and will be blowing OUT not sucking IN on the straw. Let the papers dry on a flat surface.

HAND AND FOOT TRACING

The smallest children enjoy having their hands traced on paper by an adult. Use a pretty color for the little hand, then trace your own hand next to it (or on top of it) with another color. Feet are fun to trace too. It might be fun to trace the same hand each year on a birthday, or other holiday and save them to compare the growth as it occurs. Be sure to date and label each one. If you are lucky enough to have several grandchildren, why not make a collage of all their handprints, with the names and birthdates inside each, in different colors.

## COLLAGE

Most children love to collect things and glue them down. These may be seeds, leaves, shells, snippets of ribbon or fabric, tissue paper or noodles. The possibilities are endless. You may see a theme developing as you pick up things on a walk or vacation, or when a holiday is getting near.

Here is a neat way to facilitate the process. Put a newspaper down on the work surface. Supply stiff paper or light cardboard as a base of the collage. Give the child a small amount of white glue mixed ½ and ½ with water in a jar lid or other non-tippy container. Supply Q-tips to use as glue brushes. Easy to cleanup!

## PENNY PEOPLE

Penny people are a fun way for children to start simple figure drawing. Trace around a penny for the head and the child can fill in the details of his self -portrait. Trace one for each person in the family. You may need to add a pet or two. The child can then fill in the eyes and smile and maybe hair and a body. You might want to use dimes or quarters for different sized people. It is fun to see how many details are added as the child matures.

## NOT- SQUARE SNOWFLAKES

An artist friend of mine insists that children should not be taught to fold and cut up square paper into forths to make snowflakes. They aren't supposed to be square! The nifty solution to this problem is to fold a round coffee filter into half, then thirds. Cut the top curve off straight across. Then cut notches into the edges and the outer curve. The more snippets the better the snowflake! And it has 6 sides!

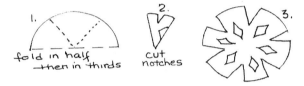

1. fold in half then in thirds

2. cut notches

3.

PAPER DOLLS

When you were a child you probably learned how to do this. Fold a half sheet of paper (4"x11") 4 times accordion style to

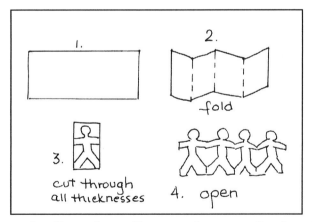

1.

2. fold

3. cut through all thicknesses

4. open

make 5 sections. Draw and cut, or freehand cut, simple girls or boys, with their hands extending into the fold on either side. Open up the paper and the dolls are all holding hands. It is fun to see how long a string of dolls you can cut, and other interesting things as well. Try hearts, pumpkins, etc. They just have to meet at the edge for it to work.

Even more fun: Draw half of two different figures holding hands. When opened, the paper will have alternating people.

EGG YOLK PAINTING

You can use store-bought or easy-mix, or your own sugar cookie recipe for the 'canvas' for these beauties  Of course it will be fun to have egg-shaped cookies to paint for Easter, and stars for Christmas, or the Fourth of July. Mix an egg yolk with a teaspoon of water. Divide between several small dishes and add enough food coloring to make bright colored paints. Using small, clean brushes you and your grandchildren can paint the cookies.

CRAYON CHIP STAINED GLASS

When the crayons are beyond saving, take off their paper wrappers; smash them up in a plastic bag, with the colors that look nice mixed together. You can put the chips in between layers of waxed paper, place the waxed paper on newsprint, and iron the layers with a fairly cool iron. The crayon chips will melt, leaving beautiful swirls of color.

An adult should handle the iron, but the children should watch the process.

SAVING THE ART WORK

You will want to save the most precious productions of course. They can't all fit on your refrigerator!! A large shallow drawer, basket, or box or a large portfolio will work. In addition to paintings and drawings, our grandchildren like to create their own greeting cards for our birthdays. These go into my lidded basket too, of course, and recently even a few handmade books.

There are picture frames available that are designed with an open side so that art can be easily changed without moving the frame. Our daughter-in-law, Cindy, keeps the boys creations current this way in their home 'gallery'.

> Bumpin' up and down in my little red wagon.
> Bumpin' up and down in my little red wagon.
> Bumpin' up and down in my little red wagon.
> Won't you be my darlin'?

# SOUNDS OF MUSIC

Children all respond to the sounds of music and rhythms. Even before they can walk babies will bounce to the beat and 'dance' in their own way. There are some wonderful tapes and CDs of music recorded for children. Some of the ones I know and love are Hap Palmer, Ella Jenkins, Pete Seeger, and Raffi. Be sure to have a tape or CD of "traveling music" in your car so you can all sing as you go.

They will love to hear your own favorite music as well. Try sound tracks of the Broadway Musicals, Dixieland Jazz, Gospel, African Rhythms, Sousa Marches, The Nutcracker Suite, or Country Western. See what makes them dance.

STRIKE UP THE BAND
Put together a simple drum set from empty containers with lids, such as coffee cans, oatmeal boxes, saltboxes, of all different sizes. Give your grandchild a dowel or chopstick for a drumstick and you join in too. Make a rattle by putting a few beans in a can with a tight lid. Have some bells you can use? Why not have a parade? Find some fun hats for everyone and march!!

## MAY I HAVE THIS DANCE?

Children often dance spontaneously to music they enjoy. If your little ones do, you might have fun adding some scarves or ribbons to wave around. Play some waltzes, salsa music, country western, and maybe tangos? Grandpas make especially good dancing partners for little ones because they can lift you up and twirl you around.

One creative grandma has a collection of tap shoes (collected at thrift shops and garage sales) in all sizes. She has group tap dancing whenever there is a family get-together! Haven't you always wanted to try it?

## SONGS TO SHARE

Do you remember these songs?

- Hokey Pokey
- I Love You (a Bushel and a Peck)
- You Are My Sunshine
- Where is Thumbkin?
- Doe, a Deer
- Oh! Susanna!
- Yankee Doodle
- Heads, Shoulders, Knees and Toes
- The Wheels on the Bus
- Waltzing Matilda

Think about all the songs you learned as a young child and I'll bet the words will come back to you, and your grandchild will learn and remember them just as you did. And you can share the fun of singing together. If she goes to pre-school, she will most likely be delighted to teach you some new songs too.

Other songs you probably know and the children love to sing are:

- I'm a Little Teapot
- Itsy Bitsy Spider
- Mary had a Little Lamb
- Pop! Goes the Weasel
- I've been Workin' on the Railroad
- Daisy, Daisy
- Home on the Range
- Twinkle, Twinkle Little Star
- Five Little Monkeys Jumpin' on the Bed
- If you're Happy and you Know it...

  o (Clap your hands,
  o Stamp your feet
  o Turn around
  o Blow a kiss)

## INSTRUMENT PETTING ZOO (AGE 5+)

Those of us who live in the San Francisco Bay Area of California are fortunate to have several excellent orchestras nearby. One orchestra we know of provides an opportunity, each season, for young children to come to the theater and (with help or course) touch, hold, and play the various instruments in the orchestra: to toot a flute or pluck a cello. What a great way to be introduced to great music!

If the orchestra is not available for hands-on experimentation, ask your talented friends if they would be willing to share and play their instruments with the children. I'll bet they would love to perform.

STATUES **(AGE 2+)**
While the music plays, all the children dance and twirl and when it stops everyone freezes into position. If there is a grownup who can play the piano or other instrument, that is ideal, but the game also works just fine with a recording or even a radio with a good music station.

## LET'S PRETEND

Little children love to pretend. And you
will too if you let yourself get into it.

TABLE CAVE
A sheet, blanket, or bedspread draped
over a table makes a great cave/
house/hideout for kids, bears, or
goldilocks.
Build a cozy house with sofa pillows for
very little ones to hide inside.

THE DRESS-
UP BOX
At our
house it is
a suitcase,
which
holds the
collection of
colorful
cast-offs.
Granny's
blouse is
just the
right length
to be a
dress. Add
belts,
scarves,
and fancy
shoes and of course hats galore. Grampa
can donate old ties, vests, shoes, hats,
and sunglasses. Why not a lace curtain for
a bride to wear?

Don't forget some beads and necklaces. A feather boa is a favorite of one grandson!

## CHAIR TRAIN

I'll bet you did this when you were a kid. Line up all the dining room chairs to make a train or bus, or airplane. Take turns being the driver (engineer, pilot) and the flight attendant (conductor). Where shall we go today? Provide simple props (hats, bags to use as luggage) and paper to make tickets.

## TEA PARTY TIME

Boys as well as girls like being invited to a party. Do include Grandpa if he is available. Also invite all the favorite dolls and stuffed critters, of course. I remember one tea party which actually had 11 guests (one Nana, one granddaughter, and 9 assorted stuffed friends!)

We like to set the smallest, low table with a little tablecloth (tea towel) and tiny cups and saucers for everyone. The'"tea" is usually pink lemonade or a weak cranberry herbal tea, and our "cookies" are little square oat cereal pieces. We also love to have grapes sometimes, or tiny Teddy Grahams. We have pretend sugar and milk so that any spills are not sticky.

### PLAYS AND PRODUCTIONS

Some kids love to make up plays and put
on "shows" for their families and friends.
Sometimes this is inspired by the dress up
box, and sometimes by a song or story
they have heard or seen. Our
granddaughters put on an annual
Christmas play. Our grandsons go for the
more physical performances, such as
gymnastics.

You may be called on to watch a rehearsal
or help write tickets or programs. And
applaud with great enthusiasm!! One four-
year-old, Eliza, acted out the 'So Long,
Farewell' scene from the Sound of Music
on the stairs with her grandparents
(wearing napkins on their heads) as the
nuns!

Some days the children will be dogs, or
cats. Other days they will be kings or
queens. Crowns are fun to make, and our
granddaughter used to love making them
for the whole family. Have child sized
scissors and construction paper and a
stapler at the ready. Glitter pens and
stickers are optional.

Royal Crowns:

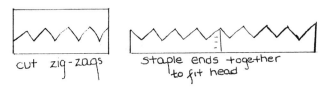

cut zig-zags        staple ends together
to fit head

Empty wrapping paper tubes can easily be
transformed into magic wands, telescopes
or swords (sword fighters must only hit
each other's swords, not bodies).  They
can also act as a tube for rolling marbles
through, and, if you close the ends with
tape can be wonderful noisemakers with a
spoonful of dried beans inside.

GRANDMA'S BEAUTY SHOP
Gather your combs, ribbons, mousse, curlers
and nail polish.  Create a spa for those little
ladies.
And for the gentlemen, a barbershop with
shaving cream and empty razors and lots of
mirrors is great fun.

PLAYING STORE
Kids love to pretend buying and selling in a
pretend toy store, grocery store, hardware
store..whatever!.  Try a family restaurant
where the kids take orders then prepare and
serve simple lunch items to eachother and
their grandparents.

FAIRY BASKETS

Can you imagine a tiny garden built for the enjoyment of a fairy? Our granddaughters had a 'fairy basket party' so they and their friends could make just such a thing.

Each child was given a small, flat-bottomed basket, and filled it about 1½ inches deep with garden dirt. Then they created an enchanted garden for the imaginary fairies, by placing tiny stepping stones, snippets of herbs and flowers, a pond in a bottle-cap, pretty stones and shells. Maybe you have some glass beads or buttons to add. Have the children tell you about what the fairies will do in their garden.

---

*We don't stop playing because we grow old
...We grow old because we stop playing.*

---

# WIGGLES AND GIGGLES
## Games for Indoors and Out

CHOOSING WHO IS "IT"
You remember this from the playground when you were young.

Put up your fists and count each fist as you say:
One potato, two potato, three potato, four, five potato, six potato, seven potato more. ('more' is out) OR add, my mother said to choose the very best one! ('one' is out)

CAN YOU RUN? **(AGE 2 +)**
A fun active game for the very youngest grandchildren, is a very simple and happy game. It goes like this. Grandma or Grandpa finds a safe spot outdoors and then gives action directions. "Can you run to the tree?" "Can you walk to the door?" "Can you run to the wall?" "Can you walk backwards to me?" "Can you jump off the bottom step?" Children love it because, of course, they CAN!

| |
|---|
| Eeny Meeny Miney Mo. Catch a tiger by the toe. If he hollers, let him go. Eeny Meeny Miney Mo |

BUBBLES **(AGE 1+)**

As soon as children can walk they love to chase bubbles. They enjoy blowing

bubbles when they are a little older, but chasing is always fun. Experiment with different wands. Some make huge bubbles, and some very tiny.

Our grandmothers blew bubbles with an empty thread spool and a saucer of soapy water.

There is bubble juice on the market now that makes very durable bubbles that can land on things without popping. We have found some still sitting around days later.

SCHOOL (ON THE STAIRS) **(AGE 3+)**
This is such a favorite at our house!! The "teacher" is usually Nana. (But can be one of the children, or Grandpa.) The children (two or more works best, but even one child with a stuffed friend is OK.) line up on the bottom step. This is "kindergarten". The teacher holds a small object, like a button, in one hand, changing from one hand to the other behind her back occasionally. She holds out her two closed fists for each child to choose which contains the button. If he chooses correctly, he gets to move up a stair to "first grade'" If he guesses wrong, he stays where he is until it is his turn again. The stairs are the grades up through high school. It works best if you have 12 stairs, but you can use what you have.

I'm thinking of something that is: ROUND !

I'm thinking of something that is RED!

I'm thinking of someone who wants a HUG!

HIDE AND SEEK

This all-time favorite is a game that even two-year olds can enjoy. Indoors or out, it can be varied slightly as the children grow. Littlest ones need to be able to find you easily and fast, and they will often hide in plain sight, just covering their eyes. As they get older the places they look and hide will become more challenging. It is a game for the whole family to enjoy. It is fun for the youngest and the oldest to team up and hide and count and search for others together. When playing outdoors with children always be sure the outer limits of the game are clear. We don't want to lose anyone!

RED LIGHT/GREEN LIGHT **(AGE 4+)**

Do this on a lawn or in a rumpus room with lots of space. Kids are at one end and whoever is "It'" at the other. Decide on the movement to be used to cross the lawn (running, hopping, crawling etc.) "It" says "Green light" and they can go as fast as possible until he says "Red Light". Then all forward motion must stop. If someone is caught moving when the light is red, they must go back to the beginning. Take turns being "It".

RHYMES WITH….. **(AGES 3 OR 4+)**

This is a good game for driving in the car, or waiting quietly. You might start with "What words can you think of that rhyme with red?" (head, bed, sled). After you all have come up with a few try, blue, then maybe black, white. etc. Orange will stump everyone. When the colors are exhausted you could go to numbers, family names, or whatever!

## TREASURE HUNT  (AGE 3+)

A treasure hunt can be great fun on many levels. For pre-readers the clues can be simple pictures to lead to the next clue. Or the child can ask for help reading. Some clever grannies write their clues in rhymes. The idea is to figure out where the next clue will be, and then the next, eventually leading to the treasure. My oldest granddaughter, Andie, is now setting up treasure hunts for her adults. The treasure can be something important, such as a birthday gift, or just a tiny treat.

## EGG HUNT (ANY AGE)

We love to do egg hunts in the spring. The eggs we use are the hollow plastic eggs that easily come apart into two pieces. A tiny goldfish cracker or a mini marshmallow can be a treat hidden in some or all of the eggs. An older child or grownup can hide the eggs in the garden or one room of the house, and the littler people, each with a small basket can look for them. Take turns hiding and finding. Be sure to count how many you are starting with, so none get forgotten.

Ring around the rosies.
Pocket full of posies.
Ashes, ashes,
We all fall down!

## DOMINOS

Older children can enjoy playing the classic forms of the dominos game, matching numbers. For the little ones, the most fun is to set up the long 'fence' made of dominos standing on end, about 1 inch from each other. The more patient you all are, and the longer you can make it (including ramps and spirals) the more fun it is to watch it fall. Let the youngest tip the one on the end.

## BALL GAMES (ALL AGES)

We like to keep several kinds of balls around the house, but it works best for us if the play is outdoors. If you have a driveway or patio, you can play bounce and catch games, basketball in a wastebasket, keep- away, soccer, variations of handball or dodgeball. Make it up to match the ages and skills of your players.

## SIMON SAYS (4+)

You remember: The person who is "it" says: "Simon says, touch your head!" Everybody touches his or her head. "Simon says, turn around!" "Simon says, blink your eyes!" "Jump up and down!" Do it and you're out! Simon needs to say it.

FOLLOW THE LEADER **(3+)**
Take turns being the leader, and all follow
along. Climb up the stairs, walk around
the chair, crawl under the table, scoot
behind the sofa, walk backwards to the
door, etc. etc.

TEDDY BEAR HOCKEY **(3+)**
We made this one up one winter day. You
need a long room or hallway with a
smooth floor. (No rug)
Choose a beany baby or another stuffed
critter who has an athletic streak and sit
about 10-12 feet away from your little
partner, with your legs wide apart. Try to
slide the toy to your opponent. More
competitive variation: try to slide it past
each other. The beany baby gets points if
he manages to get past a player. No
throwing is allowed.

HIDE THE THIMBLE **( AGE 3 OR 4+)**
This game can be as easy or as hard as
your grandchildren like it. My
grandmother called it "Hide the Thimble"
but who knows what a thimble is these
days? Any small object can be hidden
from the children, and they are helped to
find it by clues like "You are getting
hotter" as they get close to it, and "You
are getting colder now" as they move
away. Do keep the hiding places very easy
for the youngest ones. If you are hiding a
beany baby he might be found peeking
out of your pocket or sitting on your head!

MEMORY GAMES **(4+)**
This is a game for quiet times. There are
many memory games on the market,
which consist of pairs of picture cards.
Take turns turning over two at a time,
and try to remember where the matching
cards are. This can be fun played with
family photographs!

Another variation of a memory game is to
put a number of objects on a tray. The
child looks at the tray for a short time.
Cover the tray and then the child tries to
remember what is on the tray.

OTHER CLASSIC GAMES
Checkers, Chess, Cribbage, and Monopoly
and card games such as War, Crazy
Eights, Go Fish are all fun for children to
learn at the appropriate age. Some even
come in a 'Junior' version. There are some
easy games that need no number or letter
skills, such as Twister, Jenga, Pick-up-
Sticks and Candyland, which rely instead
on coordination or color recognition.
Charades is fun for most any age.

---

I like this rule: The one who wins the game gets to
clean it up and put it away.

---

## EXPLORING THE WORLD

Children love finding out about the world and how it works. Isn't that science? When you go for a walk (probably the all-time best activity for you and your grandkids) you will soon find how many interesting things there are to look at and pick up and ask questions about. Count things, collect things, compare things. Take your time.

Your garden is probably already a wonderful spot for children to explore. Do you have vegetables planted? Kids love to help pick berries, tomatoes, and herbs.

You could set aside a small plot of dirt for a child's garden. Even a large pot on a patio could act as a flower garden or tiny farm. Does it get enough sun?  Water?

The children could learn about compost and help prepare the soil. Some crops, which are especially good for kids to plant because the seeds are large and easy to handle, are
- **pumpkins**, (although they are slow to mature.) Plant the big ones and the tiny ones too. They take up quite a bit of garden space.
- **sunflowers**. They come in all sizes and can produce really spectacular results. Save the seeds for toasting, or feed them to the birds.
- **peas** are also fun for kids, as they love to open the pods and eat the peas.

- **nasturtiums** are fast growers and have bright colors and the flowers are edible.
- **strawberry** plants are decorative as well as productive.
- **pansies**, marigolds and geraniums are easy flowers to grow.

Do you have a fruit tree? Watch together as the blossoms change to little fruits and grow and mature. Kids can harvest fruit on a sturdy step stool with a basket for each person. Children love to be allowed to pick fruit and bring it in the house to be washed and eaten for lunch, or they can help make it into a pie or jam. Fruit leather (see recipe on page 13 in the cooking chapter) is another easy way to save the wonderful fresh flavor of fruit.

BIRD FEEDER

Make a simple bird feeder from a pinecone. First spread out a big sheet of newspaper. Start by spreading peanut butter (at room temperature) on all the bracts of a pinecone and then cover it with wild birdseed. Tie a bright ribbon around the top and hang it from a tree.
Or just fill a bird feeder and watch to see who comes to eat.

THE PANSY STORY

I remember this story from my
grandmother, and she got it from hers.
Find a pansy in your garden, the bigger
and more colorful the better. The story
goes like this:

"There was once an old man who had
two daughters. He married a woman
with two daughters of her own. The
new wife had a very fancy dress with
lots of velvet and an apron with
decorations. *(Gently pull off the large lower
center petal for the wife.)*

Her daughters also wanted fancy
dresses, so they got pretty velvet skirts
with aprons.
*(Pull off the petals on either side of the wife's).*

The old man's daughters had to wear
plain colored clothes, with no aprons.
*(Pull off the last two, plain colored petals.)*

The little old man had no money left
for clothes, so he sat at home with his
feet in a bucket of water!
*(The tiny little center of the flower looks just
like a little man, with a hat on, sitting on the
stem.)*

BIRD'S NESTS

If you find an abandoned bird's nest, show your grandchild the way it is made and the interesting and varied materials that have gone into making it. How do you think the bird found all those things? How could a bird build that nest without using hands? It is interesting to compare the nests of different kinds of birds too. Would you like to try making one?

BORROWING A BUG

Borrow a bug briefly in a small jar. Get a magnifying glass and check him out. How many legs does he have? How many wings? What do you think he eats? Does he have teeth?
Now let him go!

PLANTING BULBS

About Thanksgiving time, you should plan to plant your spring bulbs. A small child will enjoy having a special little pot with even one bulb in it. Put a few rocks in a clean pot. Add the bulb. Cover it with dirt. You can talk about the flower waiting inside the bulb for spring to come. Remind the child from time to time throughout the winter and watch for sprouts to appear in early spring. Water it occasionally.

> *Grandparents are for wondering*
> *with you.*
>
> Charlie Shedd

# LET'S GO! OUTINGS NEAR AND FAR

There are so many fun places to take children for an outing. <u>Parks and playgrounds</u> come to mind first, of course, and every town has some. The lawn is for running, and the <u>playground equipment</u> is for the little ones to challenge their skill and coordination in new ways. If there are ducks, you should take enough picnic food with you to share.

Many parks have free <u>band concerts</u> during the summer months. Take your grandchild to experience live music in an outdoor space that encourages dancing and jumping to the music.

<u>Throw rocks into a pond</u> or creek. What is it about little boys and rocks? Roll down a grassy hill. <u>Fly a kite.</u>

The local <u>fire station</u> is an exciting place for children to visit. Call first to see if there is a kid-friendly fireman available to talk to, and a big truck to climb on.

Most communities have a <u>train </u>to ride, and what a thrill that can be to take your grandchild on his first ride. Maybe it is a child-sized model train or maybe a full size grownup train. Even a subway or <u>rapid-transit train</u> is exciting for little ones. Read some train related books to the child in advance. Make the first trip a short one, in case it is a bit overwhelming.

Can you get to a <u>beach</u>? Children have such fun playing in the sand, collecting shells, building sandcastles and splashing in the water or just watching the waves. They don't need to be entertained, just watched carefully.

If you are lucky, you have a <u>zoo</u> to visit near your home. It is too bad the animals have to be in cages, but it gives us a chance to see them, which we might never do otherwise. Talk with your grandkids about the animals you see. "What do you think they eat?" " How do you think they talk to each other?" "Which would you like to bring home if you could?" "Where would you keep him?"

An <u>aquarium</u> is a fascinating place to take youngsters. There are wonderful books about fish to read before or after a trip, and a goldfish makes a perfect first pet.

A <u>petting zoo</u> is especially good for smaller children. They can feel the little critters, and maybe feed them a treat. Draw pictures of them when you get home.

Children should see a <u>farm</u> in action. Many farms are open to the public, especially around harvest time and <u>pumpkin patch</u> visits. You could take children to see the farm animals and barns and tractors. <u>Pony rides</u> are a special thrill for some kids, and most are appropriate for children as young as two.

Some communities have a <u>children's theater</u>. The plays are short, colorful and fun for kids, who are sometimes even invited to sit on the stage! Plan to keep a 2 and even 3 year old on your lap, as that's where they will most likely end up.

Your <u>local community center</u> has lists of children's events going on throughout the year. Check with them when you are expecting a visit from the grandkids.

We have <u>a children's fairyland</u> near our house, and the little ones love seeing the Three Little Pig's house, Red Riding Hoods' woods, Cinderella's castle, Little Boy Blue's haystack, etc.

Another kind of ferry is the <u>ferryboats</u>, which cross the San Francisco Bay. If you live in California or the northwest, your area might have commuter boats. A fairly short ride across the water is a thrill for a small person. A rowboat or canoe ride with a little one is also a treat, and don't forget the life-vests.

If your community has a <u>farmer's market</u> you have another opportunity to show your grandchildren fresh produce and talk about seasonal changes and maybe even learn to love a new vegetable!

There may be an orchard near you, which allows you to come and <u>pick your own</u> harvest of fruit, or berries. What a treat for the grandchildren to experience that!

We are fortunate to have, near our home, both a chocolate factory and a Jelly Belly factory! Check into what wonderful things are being made in your area. Most <u>Food factories</u> will have interesting tours available for the public.

<u>Camping out</u> may sound a little too complicated for some Grandparents to tackle with young children, but there are a few ideas to simplify and make it a super 'outing', if you have the equipment.

Set up a small tent on your lawn or on the family room carpet! The kids can have such fun pretending they are in the woods. Supply flashlights and let them sleepover in the tent. You can have pretend campfires, sing songs and even bring s'mores from the kitchen. (Try making them in the microwave!)

One super-grandma I know has, for years, had a real camp for her 11 grandchildren. They all go to her cabin <u>without parents</u> for a week in the summer. The kids form teams and help prepare, cook and cleanup the meals, with the older ones helping the younger. They help plan and do the craft projects as well. WOW.

Many families plan <u>family outings</u> or reunions, with all generations, in a camp-like setting to reconnect the far-flung branches of the family and let the cousins do some very important bonding. There are many wonderful commercial camps as well as state and national parks, and alumni camps. You should plan your get-together almost a year in advance to be sure you have a reservation as well as coordinating everyone's family calendars.

Share the planning of meals and activities with all ages. That's part of the fun.

> *Grandparents don't have to be smart- only answer questions like why dogs hate cats, and how come God isn't married.*

# HOLIDAY IDEAS

Sometimes the only time grandparents can spend with their grandchildren is around the major holidays. This can be a good thing and a bad thing. This is a good thing, in that the air of festivity and celebration is greatly anticipated and exciting. But it is also a special challenge, in that there is so much going on that it may be hard to find the quiet bonding time that is important. Try to keep things low key and in perspective, and focus on the meaning as well as the busy-ness of the holiday. One of my friends has her granddaughter join her in adopting a small family at Christmas time. They shop and bring food and gifts to the less fortunate.

Here are some ways to make these holidays special for the little people in the family.

## WINTER HOLIDAYS

### Cinnamon Stars

Winter holidays are so full of excitement and adventures for young children. Here is a simple and delicious-smelling decoration (not meant for eating) for children to make. Not only will these stars last for years, but the stars bring the wonderful fragrance of the holidays to your home.

You will need:
    ¾ cup cinnamon
    1 tablespoon ground allspice
    2 tablespoons ground cloves
    1 tablespoon ground nutmeg
    1 cup less 1 tablespoon warmed
    smooth applesauce

Mix the applesauce with the cinnamon
and other spices to form a stiff dough. Roll
the dough to ¼ inch thickness. Cut with
star cookie cutters (or other shapes). Make
hole in the top of ornaments with a skewer
or straw. Carefully lay the ornaments on a
rack to dry. Let dry 1-2 days until
thoroughly dry, turning occasionally.
Hang with decorative thread or ribbon.
The wonderful smell will linger for weeks.

Snowflakes
Look in the Little Artists chapter (pg 35)
for Not Square Snowflakes. These can be
painted with Q-tips as brushes and dilute
food colors as your paint. The coffee filters
absorb the liquid readily. These make
really lovely stained glass decorations.

Placemats For A Special Dinner (AGE 5+)
Choose a favorite color of construction
paper. Fold it in half so the long side is
half as long as it was, and the corners are
all even. Using your safe scissors, cut
strips an inch apart starting at the fold
and ending about 2 inches from the edge
of the paper. Cut them straight and even.

You will have about 7 strips. Now find some ribbon or cut strips of colored pictures out of a magazine to weave across the strips. Over and under, over and under.

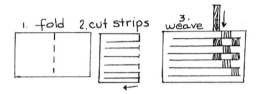

Turkey Tickets:

When the whole family gathers for Thanksgiving there are always a lot of chores that need to be done. Why not include the children in the preparations and have everyone participate. Cut out little tickets (the kids could add stickers) and write a simple chore on each one. Some chores will need more than one worker. Let each family member draw a ticket to see what he/she gets to do.

Some ideas: setting the table, making place cards, clearing the table, cutting the ends off the string beans (with blunt scissors if they are very young), pouring the ice water, reporting football scores to the group, putting whipped cream on the pumpkin pie...etc. Guide the smallest children to the appropriate chores, and leave chopping onions, etc. to the grownups.

Birdfeeders
  Look in the chapter Exploring Your World
  for directions for making a birdfeeder.
  This makes a wonderful gift for the wild
  creatures in your yard and is especially
  welcomed by birds during the wintertime.

GIFTS FOR PARENTS

  When you help the little ones make a gift
  for their parents on birthdays or holidays,
  you are teaching the joy of sharing your
  time and special talents with others you
  love. They will learn to give, not just
  receive. Here are some ideas:

Shadow Picture of Child
  Have the child sits in strong lamplight so
  that her shadow falls on the wall. Tape a
  paper on the wall to catch the entire
  shadow of her face in profile. She must sit
  VERY still. You carefully draw around the
  edge of the shadow. Cut out the silhouette
  and mount it on contrasting paper.

Cranberry Sauce
  This important addition to holiday dinners
  is very easy to make and fun to give.

  You will need:
        2 cups of water
        2 cups of sugar
        1 pound of cranberries
  In a medium saucepan, put the water and
  sugar together and cook about 5 minutes,
  stirring. Add the cranberries and cook
  gently until the skins pop. Children can
  have fun watching from a safe distance.

Cool and ladle into clean small jars, as gifts. Make pretty labels. Tie a bow.

### Hand Print or Tracing

Handprints made into Art Clay, plaster of paris or any other clay are a permanent reminder of how little these people really are. Even easier to make are painted handprints, which can be made with a strong water color or acrylic paint. Tracings (see Little Artists chapter, page 33) are quick and fun to do. Check with a local framing shop for ideas of how to frame them as gifts.

### Fabric Gifts

Using fabric crayons, children can draw designs on paper and you can iron them onto t-shirt, apron, tote bag, etc. Perfect for Mother's Day, Father's Day or a special birthday gift. You might like to add the child's name or some appropriate greeting to the shirt.

### Pomanders

These old fashioned balls of fragrance are easy and fun to make and our grandmothers probably made them as children. You need an orange and a box of whole cloves. With a toothpick, a child can poke a lot of holes in the orange, either in a line, or another design, and fill each hole with a clove, pushed in tight. The combination of orange peel and clove smells wonderful. Poke as many cloves into the orange as you can and tie with a pretty ribbon, so it can hang in the closet, or somewhere to smell nice for a long time. It will shrink a little as it dries.

HALLOWEEN TRICKS
The following are some easy and
not-very-scary projects for Halloween,
which the children can help create to
decorate your house or as gifts to take
home to theirs.

> *A grandmother pretends she doesn't*
> *know who you are on Halloween.*
>
> *Erma Bombeck*

Baby Ghosts:
I love these because they are so 'not-
scary'. You will need cotton balls and
tissues and string. Place a cotton ball in
the center of the tissue and tie the string
around the tissue to form its head. Use a
long string so you can hang them from a
tree or doorway. Add dots for eyes if
you want.

Fuzzy Spiders
For each big black spider you will need
four long black pipe cleaners and one
black pom-pom.  Simply twist the pipe
cleaners all together in the middle and
separate in to eight legs, and then glue the
pom-pom into the center to make the
head.  Bend the legs a little so the spider

has knees. If you want to hang them, tie a long black thread around the body.

Uncle Abner
This variation on a scarecrow is a life-size visitor who can sit on a porch swing, balance in a tree, hide in a bush, or even pop out of a barrel! You just collect pants, a shirt, boots, and gloves from Grandpa's closet or the ragbag and stuff him with rolled-up towels for his limbs, and a pillow for his middle. A funny rubber mask makes the best face and a hat adds realism.

VALENTINE EXTRAVAGANZA

What fun it can be to make valentines for your friends and family!

Cover your work surface with newspaper. Make a list of friends and neighbors, teachers and family members who would love a homemade valentine. You will need some pens, construction paper and other fancy kinds of paper, doilies, ribbons, stamps and stickers. Get some glue sticks and scissors. Buttons, sequins or glitter makes it even fancier.
A special addition would be a photograph of the child centered on a heart or doily.
A nice touch is to have some envelopes to enclose the final production. Here's how to cut a nice even heart:

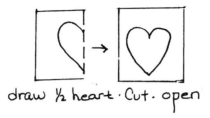

draw ½ heart · Cut · open

<u>Heart Cookies</u>
   Choose two sizes of heart cookie cutters.
Using the brown-sugar cinnamon cookie
recipe on page 13, or another favorite
sugar cookie recipe, cut out the larger of
the two hearts, and then use the smaller
cookie cutter to cut out the center of the
big heart so you have a heart-shaped
window in the cookie. The little heart can
be baked separately too of course.

Glaze them with:
      1 cup powdered sugar
      1 tablespoon milk
      1 teaspoon vanilla

Stir these together until it is smooth and
spreadable. It works well to use a small
basting brush for glazing. Sprinkle with
red white or pink sprinkles while glaze is
still wet.

Or using three graduated sizes of heart
cookie cutters, bake and cool the three
sizes of cookies and stack them to make a
pretty pile of hearts. Wrap them in red
cellophane and tie with a pretty bow.

## FOURTH OF JULY

### Melon Basket

Summer time is a traditional time for families to gather for reunions or shared vacation time. The warm weather lends itself to picnics, parades and water fights. Here is picnic idea that's festive and fun to work on with little helpers.

You will need a large, preferably seedless, watermelon. The adult can use a sharp knife to cut a slice off the bottom so it can sit securely. Then carve the lid off the top. Now the children can use melon balers to scoop out round melon balls and put them in a bowl to be used in fruit salad. See page 7 for more fruit ideas. When the melon shell is empty make pretty zig-sags or scallops around the edge and refill the melon basket with the fruit salad.

### Hats for the Parade

Make paper hats for everyone in the family. Children can help according to their age. Draw or paint red, white and blue stars and stripes on them. Stick a feather in your cap and call it macaroni!

Here is my granddaughter Andrea's recipe for paper hats:

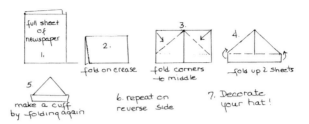

## Pinwheels

With red, white or blue construction paper, cut a square. Decorate with stars or stickers if you want. Then draw a line from corner to corner across the center. Cut from each corner to an inch from the center. Stick a pin or slender nail through every other point and then into the middle. Stick the point into a small dowel (wooden chopstick works well) or a stiff straw. Blow across it and watch it spin!

## MOTHER'S DAY

### Fancy hats

Your little ones will have fun making hats for mommy, grandmothers, and aunties too.

To prepare for this activity, gather plain dinner sized paper plates, and cut a circle 6 inches in diameter out of the center of each. Poke two holes on opposite sides of the plate and tie a ribbon into each. These will tie under the chins, to keep the hat on. Gather bows, flowers, buttons, ribbons scraps of lace and let the youngsters decorate each chapeau. (Let the glue dry before trying on the hat!)

## Acknowledgements

I hope you enjoy using this book as much
as I have enjoyed writing it, with lots of help
and ideas from good friends and family.

I especially want to acknowledge and thank
Sally, Becky, Jackie, Carole, Inez, Joan,
Jill, Faye, Leslie, Sheri, Charlotte, Nancy,
Mary, and Christina and most especially
my husband Fred.

My son Brian is my technical guru. Thanks
to all of you.

# Notes